HOW TO MEET
NEW PEOPLE
GUIDEBOOK

Overcome Fear
and Connect Now

KEITH & TOM "BIG AL" SCHREITER

How To Meet New People Guidebook
© 2017 by Keith & Tom "Big Al" Schreiter

Published by Fortune Network Publishing
PO Box 890084
Houston, TX 77289 USA

Telephone: +1 (281) 280-9800

BigAlBooks.com

ISBN-10: 1-948197-07-3
ISBN-13: 978-1-948197-07-6

CONTENTS

PREFACE

This book is for shy or introverted people who want to get better at meeting new people. We want to know how to:

1. Meet new people.

2. Start conversations safely.

That's it.

Later we can learn about rapport, selling our ideas, how to bond for the long-term, make friends, or become a world-class public speaker.

But for now, we want a commonsense approach to meeting new people and starting a conversation.

What if you already know how to meet an unlimited number of people and start awesome conversations?

Well, if you already knew these skills, you wouldn't be reading this book. You would be out talking to new people!

But for the rest of us? We want to overcome our fear of talking to strangers. We want to feel comfortable, even if we are at a party or event where we don't know anyone.

We can be great at meeting new people. This book will give us the step-by-step techniques.

—Keith and Tom "Big Al" Schreiter

I travel the world 240+ days each year.
Let me know if you want me to stop in your
area and conduct a live Big Al training.

→ **BigAlSeminars.com** ←

FREE Big Al Training Audios

Magic Words for Prospecting

plus Free eBook and the Big Al Report!

→ BigAlBooks.com/free ←

I WANT TO MEET NEW PEOPLE NOW, BUT ...

Are we nervous when meeting people? Do we feel a lack of self- confidence? Are we afraid of rejection?

Of course. These feelings mean we are normal.

We get these feelings because of our past. Do we have vivid memories of stupid mistakes in grade school? Maybe we humiliated ourselves in front of the class. Everyone has embarrassing mistakes from their past.

What happens when we relive those memories in our mind? Our mind feels as though those mistakes are happening to us again. This chips away at our self-confidence.

Or, maybe we remember our parents saying, "Don't talk to strangers!"

Now, our parents gave us this program with the best intentions. In our early years, this program served us well. But what about now?

Now our program to avoid talking to strangers holds us back. We have a nagging feeling in our minds that we shouldn't approach strangers.

So, if we haven't practiced the skills of meeting new people, it would be natural for us to feel shy and uneasy about our encounters.

If we feel uneasy talking to strangers, we have good reasons.

To counteract these negative feelings, we need to have new, positive experiences of talking to people. To do this, we will need new skills.

Skills?

Yes. Like any task in life, meeting new people requires skills. Fortunately, we can learn new skills. We learned how to use a smartphone. We learned how to manipulate the remote control for our televisions. Meeting people will be one more skill we can add to our experience.

With a little practice, we will remove our fears and increase our success.

The first attempt at getting a date.

Imagine a 15-year-old boy asking a young lady for his first date. Yes, we know this will be ugly. We hope the young lady will have mercy on him as he stutters and fails to get to the point. Thankfully, most young ladies have manners and compassion.

What happens if we never attempt to meet new people? Then our first encounter will look similar to the 15-year-old boy's experience. We will be nervous, insecure, and will speak with hesitation.

But let's fast-forward one year. The young boy asked for many dates during the past year. Each request was an improvement, and of course, he got better results. His confidence went up. Now he knows what to expect and how to answer most responses. And yes, he will get more dates.

We will get better.

The more we practice, the easier it gets. The first few attempts at meeting new people are the most difficult.

A good analogy to this is drinking coffee. If we are coffee lovers, we can't wait to have our next cup of coffee. But was it that way the first time we tasted coffee?

No. Our first taste of coffee made us think, "Oh, this is bitter. But other people like it. I will keep trying until I like it."

It is the same when we attempt to meet new people. We have to remember that this will get easier and more successful in time. Eventually, it will become addictive.

Addictive?

Yes. When we master the skills of meeting new people, we will want to do it over and over again. We will enjoy the feeling of mastery and competence. Our fears will go away. Why? Because we will know exactly what to say and what to do when we meet new people.

Fear of failure?

Understandable. No one wants to fail. The good news is that if we mess up with one person, we have seven billion more people to choose from. It is not like we will run out of potential new people to talk to.

This is the logical viewpoint.

But what is the reality inside our heads? We think civilization will collapse if we get rejected. We don't want to make a mistake when approaching people. We don't want to feel embarrassed. We hate the thought of what other people may think or say to us.

This is the voice inside our heads. The logical viewpoint is nice. But the reality is that we want to make sure our social skills are good enough, so we won't fail.

Yes, we have anxiety about meeting new people. But, do other people care about our personal anxiety? No. They don't know about the personal drama inside our heads. So, if they don't care, it will be up to us to take our first step.

Self-talk?

We talk to ourselves all the time. Each time we talk to ourselves, our subconscious mind pays attention. If we want to become more confident talking to people, what should we say to ourselves?

Try this. "I want to meet and talk to other people." Or, "I am curious about other people and their lives." Our subconscious mind will remember these words.

We must stop telling ourselves, "I am shy. I am afraid to approach other people."

Want to feel better about meeting new people instantly?

Here is a quick way to forget about our insecurities. Think about others. We can't have two thoughts in our minds simultaneously. This way we can't be thinking about ourselves and our insecurities. Our "thinking about others" thought will dominate.

How do we do this? Think, "Oh, there is someone in this group that needs me. Someone who is shy, and hopes someone will talk to them."

Concentrate on others and we won't have to worry about our negative self-talk making us feel bad.

Still hesitant to start?

We can learn.

If others know how to connect with people, then why can't we learn how also?

It is possible. Others prove it.

Right now we lack confidence because we have a lack of experience. Let's get that experience quickly, but with the safety of a few tips from this book.

We can do it. Here is proof.

Grab a piece of paper. Write down five things we have achieved in our lives. For example, our list might look something like this:

- Learned to walk.
- Learned to drive a car.
- Graduated from high school.
- Learned how to speak basic Spanish.
- Learned how to use a computer.

Everyone has a list of accomplishments. Let's add the skill of meeting new people to our list.

JUDGMENT DAY.

Do people prejudge us?

Yes. All the time.

Does this mean that people are shallow and make immediate judgments about us? Yes.

But there is a reason they make judgments about us before they know us. The reason is survival.

We have programs that help us to survive. We don't take chances with unknown people. Could this person be dangerous? Could this person be a threat? We need to sort this out immediately. Our survival could be at stake.

Consider this scenario. I approach you wearing a hockey mask and wielding an axe. Are you starting to get a bad feeling? Are you prejudging me? I hope you are.

What are the criteria that people use to prejudge us?

We meet people. They don't know our background, we don't have a recommendation from a friend, and no one else told them about us.

So how will they judge us?

1. Body language. They will pick up hints, both obvious and subtle, from our body language. Fortunately, if we are sincere in our intentions, our body language will reflect it. We don't have to become a body language expert to meet new people.

2. The tone of our voice. We don't have to be a ventriloquist, but we should be conscious of our voice. If we have bad intentions, our voice may reflect that. Since we have good intentions, our voice should be okay.

3. The words we choose to say. We will spend most of our time in this book on the words we choose to say. Fortunately, we are in control of this also. If we choose better words, we will get better results.

And then?

That was quick. Instant judgment. It is over.

Is it unfair that people judge us this quickly? Absolutely! But it is the reality.

Ah, but there is a silver lining in these shallow, instant judgments; we only have to be impressive for a few seconds. That won't be hard to learn.

If we pass this initial judgment screening, the going gets easy. We will learn to smile, listen better, and make our conversations interesting and memorable. This could be the making of many new friendships.

Meeting new people isn't hard. It is a skill that we can learn and use for the rest of our lives.

How should we act? Here's a starting point.

Think about the people we've already met. Make a list of things we like about these people, and a list of things we don't like. For example, our "things we like" list could include things such as:

- Smiles.
- Offers to shake hands.
- Never criticizes.
- Is interested in what we say.

Example of our "things we don't like" list could include things such as:

- Bad breath.
- Avoids eye contact.
- Talks too much.
- Interrupts people.
- Tells other people they are wrong.
- Argues.
- Looks at other people as they walk by while we are talking.
- Stands too close to our face.

We will learn to be great at meeting new people.

For now, let's remember that there are three factors people use to judge us.

1. Body language.

2. Tone of voice.

3. The words we say.

These are the basics of our interactions with others. We will look at these three basic factors first. Then, we will spend the rest of this book taking our skills to a higher level.

Let's start now by learning how to improve our body language.

Body language.

How important is body language when approaching someone new? Think of someone flirting. Or, imagine someone shaking an angry fist. How about a punch in the nose?

Yes, body language makes a difference.

Do we have to be a full-fledged expert on body language to approach new people? No.

A little common sense is all we need.

Body language works two ways.

1. We need to be aware of someone else's body language.

2. When we meet new people, we want to be aware of our body language. We want to look "open" and non-aggressive. We don't want our personal body language to hurt our chances of making a new friend.

Body language is always happening. Let's deal with it.

Don't believe everything we hear.

There is an urban legend that 93% of communication is nonverbal (body language and tone of voice). It is not true.

However, people repeat this urban legend so often that many people believe it to be true.

So don't panic. We don't have to learn all kinds of strange poses and body contortions to meet new, exciting people.

The good news is that our body language generally reflects our true intentions. If we are sincere, we should do fine.

Let's focus on some commonsense basics.

Look first.

We will feel better if we can evaluate other people's body language. If someone smiles and seems open, we can reasonably expect a stress-free conversation.

Other people may look like they're in a bad mood. We don't know what happened to them earlier that day.

Some signs are obvious. For example, if someone is talking on his phone, it is a bad time to start a conversation. We wouldn't want to interrupt someone's personal conversation with a friend. Common sense rules.

We need to be careful about pre-judging.

Body language is subjective. A certain stance could have different meanings depending on the context. For instance, when we talk to a stranger, notice the stranger's stance. If this stranger is shifting weight from one leg to another, not standing still, what could that mean? It could mean:

- This stranger is not interested in our conversation and wants to leave.

- This stranger is nervous, and feels intimidated by our presence.

- This stranger recently bought uncomfortable new shoes.

- This stranger is standing on an ant hill and the ants are starting to bite!

So, we don't want to take one example of body language and make that a rule for every person in every situation.

If we've known someone for a long time, we have a baseline for their body language. When they do something different with their body, we have a better idea what it means.

But we are meeting new people. We don't have that luxury. For beginners, we should just notice the broader, more obvious signals.

Body language is a lot easier to decipher with dogs than with humans. Dogs don't have a lot of complex things going through their minds. When they are wagging their tails, it's a safe bet that they're happy.

In the human world, circus clowns and mimes have very expressive body language. Engineers and accountants have much less.

Body language will give us general information about the state of mind of the person we are talking to.

What are some easy body language hints and basics we should look for when approaching potential new friends?

Easy body language basics.

Before we approach that next stranger, we will want to perform a quick body language scan to make sure now is a good time. This is not hard. We already do this automatically. But now, we will be a bit more deliberate. Here are some obvious checkpoints.

Smile.

If the person is smiling and seems relaxed, we can safely guess that now is a good time.

But what kind of smile should we show to others?

When smiling, don't make it a forced smile. People notice that and will make negative judgments. Smiling with very tight lips that hide our teeth sends out the wrong signals. It appears that we are holding back our true feelings. And, our true feelings are not to smile.

The tight-lipped smile is better than shouting out our negative feelings, but not much better.

Instead, we want to show a genuine smile.

If we are not a gifted natural-smile person, here is a shortcut. Think happy thoughts.

Think of a scene from a happy movie. Or, picture our favorite dessert.

And if that doesn't work, visualize this: "Our boss losing the key to the office on Friday morning and announcing that everyone has to go home early for the weekend."

What if all we can do is make a half-smile, or a smirk? This might signal that we aren't sure if we should smile or not. This isn't ideal. But, on a positive note, at least we are halfway to a sincere smile.

Not sure of our smile? A little practice in front of a mirror will help. Notice the difference between that sincere smile and that fake smile. Others will read our body language, too.

Personal space.

If we unknowingly invade the personal space of people, what kind of reaction should we expect? Notice how they keep backing away from us. Or perhaps they turn away from us slightly while we are talking to them. We are making them uncomfortable. Unfortunately, few people will tell us that we are standing too close to them.

What kind of person violates personal space? The person who doesn't know he is doing it!

We must notice and be aware of this on our own. Observe people talking. Watch the body language or facial expression of the listener.

If the listener tries to change the space, that is a sign that he is uncomfortable.

In addition, some cultures have different personal space boundaries. If we want to be safe, err on the side of standing too far away.

Eyes.

There is an old saying that the eyes are the windows to one's soul. Yes, eyes do give us some clues.

Generally, when people are bright-eyed, they are happy. When they furrow their brows, and make their eyes smaller, that's not a good sign for us. These people could be worried or have some negative things on their minds.

If we have great eyesight (or we are uncomfortably too close) we might see the size of the pupils of people's eyes. Open and wide pupils are good. Of course, they would also have open and wide pupils if they just exited a dark room. Common sense, remember?

Should we look into people's eyes when talking to them? Sometimes.

Avoiding eye contact with the person we are talking to is creepy. But staring constantly, without blinking, into someone's eyes is even more disturbing. A little balance is more socially acceptable. A good way to feel good while looking into someone's eyes? Try taking inventory of their eye color, or how they use eye shadow, or even the eyebrow trim. This keeps our minds busy so that we stop thinking about what others are thinking of us.

If someone is avoiding eye contact with us, our conversation is not going well. This is a pretty obvious sign to let the other person move on. This person has other things going on that are more important than us at this moment.

Think about it. If we are talking to someone, and they keep looking at something else, how do we feel? We think, "This person finds almost everything more interesting than me."

Shifty eyes? This could signal disinterest. Our conversation partner doesn't want to be in this conversation. Maybe we are boring or our conversation partner has something else pressing. But one thing is for sure, his mind is moving much faster than we are talking. There is something else going on.

So, if we are talking to someone, we should make sure we don't have shifty eyes.

Rolling one's eyes? This may signal disbelief in what the other person is saying. Or, this could mean exasperation. For instance, a person could be thinking, "Oh my! I finally get invited to a party and now I am stuck listening to you!"

Fortunately, people don't roll their eyes often.

And finally, we must avoid scanning someone from head to toe with our eyes like a piece of hanging meat. This makes anyone feel uncomfortable.

Eyebrows.

What about the eyebrows? Can they give us clues? Sure.

We naturally notice that raised eyebrows signals friendliness. This means someone is thinking, "Hey, you are okay." Sometimes people unconsciously give us a quick eyebrow flash. Feel good when that happens. It is a good sign.

And furrowed eyebrows? Caution. This is the verbal equivalent of saying "no" to us or to what we are saying. We should wait for a better time to approach this person.

Women can communicate an entire language with the movements of their eyebrows. Men? We are still evolving. Don't expect the same level of expressiveness.

Crossed arms.

When we see someone with their arms crossed, our first thoughts are to stay away. This person looks protective or wishes to show authority. Maybe they don't agree with us or feel threatened by the situation.

This could be true.

But remember, a single body language signal could mean many different things. For example, folded arms could also mean:

- The person is cold.
- The person is nervous and wants to hide his or her shaking hands.
- The person could be hiding a missing button on his or her shirt.
- The person wants to relax and this is a comfortable position.
- Or, this man doesn't have six-pack abs, but 24-pack abs instead. This is a good place to rest his arms.

So how do we know what this person wants to project to others? Check this person's face. Or check their eyes. Look for other clues to help us determine if this is a safe person to approach.

Nodding.

It is no secret that nodding means approval. A gentle up-and-down motion will do. We don't want to look like a bobble-head toy.

When people talk to us, they enjoy the feeling of acceptance or agreement with our occasional nod.

Shaking hands.

People don't naturally shake hands with enemies. Extending our hand for others to shake is a great body language signal. It shows others that we like them and wish to meet them.

When extending our hand, make sure our palm is not pointing down. This could send negative signals. Instead, make sure our palm is pointing out to the side, or better yet, pointed slightly up. This is a more "open" position and signals friendliness.

Other body language signs.

What if someone is rubbing their chin?

Instinctively we know that they are thinking of what we said. The good news is that they were listening to us. We should feel great about this.

What if someone is tapping their fingers on the table or desk while we are talking? There's a good chance they've lost interest in what we are saying, or we are taking too long to get to the point.

Shrugging shoulders? Depending on our relationship, this could mean anything from "I don't care" all the way to "Why are we having this conversation?"

Checking his or her watch or looking at a clock? Hmm. Somebody wants to be somewhere else at this moment.

Make sure our body language is good.

For example, do we look tired? That is not good. Do we look like we are full of energy and happy to be where we are? That is better.

To get a more animated look, we could do some jumping jacks or calisthenics before meeting people. Exercising our bodies tells our brains to be excited. The people we meet are reactive. They will react positively to our excitement and animation.

This starts a great feedback loop. When they have positive reactions to us, we react to them by being friendlier. Then, they react to our friendliness … and, well, we get the point. Endless positive feedback loops are wonderful.

But we just want to meet new people, right?

We don't want to be a body language researcher. However, a quick look at body language before approaching someone is helpful.

Let's make it simple.

1. We want to watch for happy signals.

2. We want to watch for unhappy signals.

That's it!

We don't want to meet closed-minded or angry people. The good news is that we can choose the people we approach.

A quick personal body language checklist before approaching new people?

1. Smile.

2. Don't furrow our eyebrows.

3. Be sincere, and the rest of the body parts take care of themselves.

4. And maybe add a breath mint.

Our voice.

The second factor people use to prejudge us is our voice. Now, we are not ventriloquists. It will be hard to disguise our natural voice for very long. For now, we are stuck with it. But, here are a few hints that will help.

Speed of voice.

Some people talk very fast. Others talk very slow.

Do we want to make others feel comfortable?

Then attempt to talk more at their natural speed. If they talk very fast, and we talk very slow, their mind wanders. Boring! They become anxious between words. They finish our sentences. They want to give us caffeine to speed us up.

We will increase our normal speaking speed for these people, so they won't become stressed.

What about people who speak more slowly?

If we talk too fast to these people, they too will feel stressed. They won't trust us. They feel that we are trying to sneak information past them. When we slow down, we see the stress released from their faces.

It is easier for people to trust us when we match their talking speed.

Tone of voice.

Our tone of voice can override the meaning of our words. Yes, we could say the correct words, but our voice has to match our meaning of the words. Here is an example.

Say the word "okay" with the following different tones of voice:

- Sarcastic.
- Enthusiastic.
- Angry.
- Bored.
- Loud. (You know, that outside voice our mothers told us not to use indoors.)
- Scared.
- Kindly.

There is a difference, right? In the next chapter we will start learning the words to say, but saying words in a kind tone of voice makes a difference.

Do we have to take voice lessons to get our tone correct? No. Usually our tone reflects our intentions. The solution is to have good intentions.

How we say things matters.

People are terrible listeners. They may not remember what we say, but they will remember how we said it. How we say things can make people feel better or worse. Of course, we want them to feel better.

Is now a good time to talk?

Finally, choose good timing. Nothing ruins conversations like bad timing. Some examples of bad timing when approaching people? When they are:

- Busy or stressed.
- Reviewing voice messages on their phones.
- Already engaged in an intense personal conversation.
- Getting in their car.
- Putting food in their mouths.

When we are considerate of others, our timing should be perfect.

Now, let's get to the third criteria people use to prejudge us, the words we say. Improving this skill will give us self-confidence. Plus, we will be more effective when we meet new people.

What do I say first?

What would we want to start our conversation with?

Try the word, "Hi."

"Hi" is not too hard to remember, and it is a socially acceptable word. Since people are reactive, they will automatically reply with, "Hi." Now the conversation has started.

Whew! The hardest part is over.

What if they don't say "Hi" back? Easy. We are done with this conversation. Time to move on. No need to continue.

What do we do after people say "Hi" in return?

We have many options depending on the situation. Let's take a look at the most obvious words we could say next.

Ask a simple question. Why? Because people have to respond to our questions. We call this … conversation.

Here are some easy questions to ask:

- "How are you?"
- "What is your name?"
- "Do you have a moment?"

- "Do you know where the toilets are located?"
- "Have you been in line long?"
- "Am I in the right line?"
- "Are you enjoying this nice day also?"
- "Are you waiting also?"
- "Do you know the host of this party?"
- "Do you need help with the door?"
- "Can I help you with those packages?"
- "What's that book you are holding?"
- "Where are you traveling from?"

Are questions the only way to continue our conversation? No. We could make comments also. Here are some examples:

- "Nice shoes."
- "Our line is really long."
- "What well-behaved children you have."
- "That snack looks delicious."
- "It sure is crowded here today."

Social basics.

Imagine we are at a party. We approach someone standing alone. After saying "Hi," we don't want to seem weird by starting with invasive questions.

What are invasive questions? Here are some examples:

- "How much money is in your bank account?"

- "What time do your children leave your house for school in the mornings?"
- "Are those your real teeth?"
- "Had any operations lately?"

Okay, just kidding. Not only are these questions invasive, they are also creepy.

When meeting someone new at a party, we want to keep the conversation easy, safe, and light-hearted. People may feel reluctant to open up to a stranger in the first few seconds.

So after "Hi," our conversation might sound like this:

"What is your name?"

Not too bad. No one at a party would be offended by that.

Could we make this conversation easier for our conversation partner? Try saying this instead:

"Hi. My name is Keith. What is your name?"

Why is this more comfortable? Because we offered our name first. This makes people feel a bit more relaxed with us. We showed our new conversation partner that we are open to talking by volunteering information first.

At parties, there is a common sequence of questions that we can ask. Here they are:

- "What is your name?"
- "Where are you from?"
- "What kind of work do you do?"

Nothing invasive here. People hear these questions all the time. No one should be on edge or nervous about them.

These familiar questions relax our conversation partners. In time, we can ask deeper, more meaningful questions.

Adjust to your area.

Listen to others talk before talking. In certain areas, there will be a different social sequence of questions. For example, in Minnesota, when talking to someone, you have to ask which road they took, and how long it took them to arrive. It is a requirement.

In England? Oh my. There appears to be some sort of law that we have to talk about the weather … endlessly. Why? I don't know. The weather never changes. It is always miserable and getting worse.

Okay, a slight exaggeration. England does have good weather once or twice a year, sometimes in the afternoon. Few people have observed this, but it was reported. (Well, this is the American viewpoint anyway.)

If we attend a farmer's convention, we have to report the last time it rained, and how much.

If we attend a sales convention, we must comment on the woes of the economy and why people can't buy.

The point is, this is an easy way to start a conversation and fit in at the same time.

Starting with no agenda.

When we meet new people, they are naturally a bit defensive. They look for clues in our faces, our body language, and our words. They automatically think:

"Why are you starting this conversation? Are you truly interested in me, or do you have an ulterior motive? Should I be extra careful and guarded if I talk to you? Will this cost me money? Will you try to ask a favor?"

Yes, our internal survivor program protects us 24 hours a day. People are programmed to be cautious.

That is the bad news.

Ready for some good news?

People want to talk to us.

More specifically, they want to talk **at** us. Most people's idea of a conversation is, "A monologue about me."

Everyone loves talking about themselves. They look forward to people asking them questions. We will be the highlight of their day. Their boss doesn't listen to them. Their family doesn't listen to them. Their friends ignore them. We could be the superstar that made their month!

These are the basics of starting a conversation.

It may be a pretty boring start, but at least we started.

Now, if we want to be boring, forgettable, and to quickly fade from someone's memory, this would be the limit of our conversation.

But we want others to remember us, don't we? We want interesting conversations with people. We want to not only meet new people, but create new friends too, right?

But, we made progress.

With natural body language, a reasonable tone of voice, and a few safe questions ... surprise! We are meeting new people.

It isn't that hard. With minimum competency, we can do this.

But who wants to be the minimum? Not us. We want to overcome our fear of meeting new people and take our conversations and relationships to higher levels.

Onwards to getting better!

Can we control other people's actions?

Yes.

People are reactive. They go through life on autopilot, reacting to their internal programs.

Want to see this in action?

When we say "Hi" to someone, what do we expect back? The person normally reacts by saying, "Hi."

When we smile at someone, what do we expect back? The person smiles back.

Humans don't think about these reactions. They simply react.

So, we should think, "The behavior of people is only a reaction to what we say and do."

The $100 test.

In the parking lot, we see a stranger and give him $100. Will the stranger react? Certainly! The stranger says, "Wow! I won the lottery! By the way, do you have any more money that you can give me?"

Yes, we can expect this reaction to our $100 gift.

Now, imagine this. Instead of giving that stranger $100, what if we gave the stranger a hard punch in the nose? Will that stranger react? Yes!

The stranger says, "Oh, that was rude." (Or he possibly has a more aggressive response.)

The point is, we met the very same stranger. This stranger had two totally different reactions based upon what we did.

So yes, people do react to what we say and do.

Great news! That means our interactions with new people will be within our control. We should adopt the attitude that our outcome when meeting new people is within our control. It's a liberating feeling!

We are in control of our social interactions.

We must take personal responsibility for our social interactions. We can't depend on others. What happens if we go to a social event, and stand like lost sheep against the wall or in the corner? That means we are depending on someone else to rescue us. That rescue may not come.

That is why we should make the first move and approach someone. By remembering that people react to what we say and do, we can feel confident that our attempt to meet someone new will have a great chance of success.

FINDING THE COURAGE TO ATTEMPT OUR FIRST CONVERSATION.

Want to know a secret?

Knowledge is power. We will learn something that will make conversations a breeze. This little fact can give hope to even the shyest, most awkward, introverted, socially-handicapped person.

Want to know the secret?

"People don't care about us."

Huh? That's the secret?

Yes.

People care about themselves.

Remember, we are talking about strangers that we wish to meet. We are not talking about people we know already. Of course, our relatives and friends are concerned about us. Well, a few are, anyway.

But strangers? Nope. Their attention is entirely on themselves. They are their favorite subject. If we make a huge mistake when talking to them, they might go home and tell their friends, but the next day they will have forgotten us.

So the good news is that we don't have to feel awkward or self-conscious. Remember, people are not thinking or caring about us. We are not that important.

Whew! That is a relief.

But other people are natural connectors.

Let's face it. Some people are better than others when meeting new people. Fortunately, we are not in competition with seven billion other humans.

Right now, we might be thinking, "I am not very good at meeting new people and making new friends. 99% of the people I know are better at this."

That could be true.

But when meeting new people, we are only in competition with ourselves. Our goal is to improve our current set of skills for meeting people.

We should compare today with yesterday. Are we getting better? If the answer is yes, we should feel good. We want to make progress towards learning these people skills every day.

But … I am shy and introverted.

An estimated one-third of all people feel this way. We are not alone. That's over two billion people who haven't mastered the skill of meeting new people comfortably. Okay, we are not the majority, but there sure are a lot of us.

But think about this. If one-third of the people we meet are shy, just like us, talking to these people will be easy. We have shyness in common. Instant bonding.

Now, we won't fix our shyness problem with some motivational quote posted on our social media page. Learning better skills and using them to build confidence is a much better solution to our shyness problem.

Is there a shortcut so I can at least get started?

Yes, and it is easy.

See that shy stranger? Think this: "I want to improve this person's day."

Maybe we can help the shy stranger talk about his favorite subject. Or, help him focus on something positive in his life.

How will that person feel? He will like us, of course.

And in the future, this person will seek us out. This person will enjoy having conversations with us. It could be the beginning of a friendship. Plus, when this person talks to others, our reputation will grow as a great conversationalist.

But ... what if I am a failure at meeting new people?

If we are afraid of contacting new people now, we are already a failure at this skill.

It can only get better when we take action. The question we should be asking ourselves is, "Am I ready to get better at this now?"

But before we rush out to meet new people, let's learn a few conversation skills. This way we will feel more comfortable in our initial conversations.

Later, we will learn where to find great people to meet.

EMPATHY.

Master empathy. Then, meeting new people is easy.

Q. What is a good way to understand empathy?

A. Put ourselves inside the other person's brain.

When we see things from other people's viewpoints, it is easy to connect. Conversations are easy. Rapport seems effortless.

Everyone thinks they are right.

My friend, Richard Brooke, says this:

"As humans, we are incredibly closed-minded and arrogant. We actually believe that what we think is the truth is TRUE, and that what someone else believes is just THEIR OPINION. This arrogance and foolishness sticks us with our beliefs, blinding us to any other possibilities - possibilities that may propel us toward success."

Okay, we think we are right.

Our viewpoint is the correct viewpoint.

What we believe is true.

Sounds pretty natural, doesn't it?

But wait. We want to meet this new person across the room. What is he thinking?

Yep. He is thinking the exact same thing. He knows his viewpoints and beliefs are correct.

Want to connect?

We love people who:

#1. Think the same way we do.

#2. Or, at least respect, honor, and allow us to think differently.

First, the easy part.

If we approach the person across the room, and he thinks the same way we do … connecting will be effortless and automatic.

Now comes the hard part.

If we approach a new person across the room, and he doesn't think the same way we do, we will have to train ourselves to respect, honor, and allow him to think differently. We need to prepare ourselves to allow different viewpoints.

Don't tell people they are wrong.

Early in my career, I felt obligated to correct the inaccurate or stupid viewpoints of other people. No one wanted to talk to me. It took me some time to figure out why people avoided talking to me.

People don't want us to correct them. People hate it when we tell them they are wrong.

If we want to meet new people successfully, we can't correct their inaccuracies and misguided opinions. We have to bite our tongues and smile. This is not comfortable to do in the beginning, but over time, we become more mellow about this.

Are people often wrong? Sure. Should we help them by pointing out their errors? No.

First, they won't listen to our corrections. Second, they will hate us for it. Enough said.

Once I stopped correcting other people's inaccuracies, conversations went much better. People liked me. I made many more new friends and contacts.

People want approval. They don't want criticism.

The more we can accept and approve of other people's viewpoints, the more attractive we become as a conversation partner. Think about our own experiences. Do we like it when people tell us that we are wrong? No.

Look at the people we currently associate with. They have many of the same viewpoints that we do. That is why we like being with them.

So why are other people wrong so often?

Well, they are not wrong.

People have different viewpoints, beliefs, and biases based upon their past experiences. For example, maybe we've experienced 30 years of happy married life. We have a certain viewpoint on marriage.

The next person we talk to? Maybe he is suffering through divorce #7. All of his divorces were contentious and ugly. Does that person have a different viewpoint or opinion on marriage? Of course!

When we talk to this new person, it is not that we are right and he is wrong. Instead, we should try to understand different viewpoints based upon different experiences.

Most people are not wrong. They look at life through the lens of different past experiences, biases, and the programs given to them while growing up. Yes, our world looks different to others.

But what if people are obviously wrong?

Okay. That happens. Some people we meet will insist the earth is flat, aliens have already landed on earth, and every known fact is part of a conspiracy theory. Maybe there are only a few of those people, but they do seem to move around a lot. We encounter them more frequently than we would like.

The rule for dealing with people who are obviously wrong? The same. Don't disagree. We don't get bonus points for playing the role of the "stupid police."

No one likes to be told they are wrong. The best way to understand this feeling is to experience it. Ready?

We are at a social gathering and meet a new person named Jeff. This is our conversation.

Jeff: "Nice to meet you too. So, how do you feel about the new mayor?"

Us: "Not bad. If the majority elected him, we should give him a chance."

Jeff: "What? Only perverts, serial killers, and psychopaths support this soon-to-be plague to humanity. So which one of these degenerate groups do you belong to?"

Us: "Uh ..."

Not a very good feeling, is it? When people disagree, we feel that they are attacking not only our judgment, but also our character.

How do we avoid these embarrassing encounters when we meet people?

By allowing them to voice their opinions, while keeping our opinions to ourselves. No one cares about our opinions anyway. People don't have room in their brains for other people's interests. Yes, slightly overstated, but people do have a full-time job thinking about themselves.

So, what should we do when people voice an opinion grossly different than ours? Well, we don't want to lie and say we agree with them. Instead, we can tactfully say, "Interesting. I never looked at it that way."

Then, let our conversation partner continue.

What if our conversation partner insists that we offer our opinion first? We can tactfully say, "Wow. There is a lot to say about that. Where should we start?"

Our conversation partner can't resist the chance to talk more. He will take over the conversation again at this opportunity. Now, we are safe. We only have to listen.

How to practice empathy.

While in public, pick out an individual to observe. For example, let's say you are sitting in the shopping mall food court. A man is frowning at his food, shouting at his children, and has a scowl on his face. We could ask ourselves, "What happened to this man before he came to the shopping mall? Did a dog bite him? Did his children wake him up early? Did someone sneeze on his food?"

Something in the man's immediate past caused this man to react negatively. We don't know what it was. We are just guessing. But we now understand that his viewpoint on a day at the shopping mall is vastly different from our viewpoint.

Next, we see a lady with her three little daughters. Everyone is happy and having a great time. Let's imagine what has happened to them. Maybe they were looking forward to the family outing. Or, possibly the food vendor gave them free food. But we do know that this second group sees the day at the shopping mall through an entirely different lens.

Let's go to a sporting event. We see a person who has painted his face in his team's colors. He lives and dies on the outcome of each play in the game.

Why does he feel this way? Maybe in grade school a team member spoke to his class. Later, that team member bought ice cream for everyone in the class.

His viewpoint on life? The world revolves around the fortunes of his favorite sports team.

And, we don't like his team.

But we don't have to bring that up in conversation. We can simply appreciate his viewpoint that his team is the best team ever in the history of humanity.

In time, we will find it easy to appreciate other people's viewpoints. Empathy comes with practice.

Plus, this exercise gives us one more benefit. By observing other people's body language over time, we will know the type of people to avoid when meeting new people. Some people are aggressive or extremely defensive. These types of people are not good candidates for conversation, especially when we are just starting out in our quest to meet people.

Appreciate, not accept.

Empathy means we appreciate their viewpoint. We understand why they might think that way.

Empathy does not mean we have to personally accept their viewpoint as the ultimate truth. It is okay in life that people think differently about things. Our mission in life is not to get everyone to think the same way we do.

What happens when there is little or no empathy?

Observe two political parties. Each party thinks the other party is 100% wrong about every issue. No cooperation. No appreciation. No allowance for different viewpoints. Pretty awful, isn't it?

This is not a good model for meeting and connecting with new people.

That negative encounter with a new person.

Even with our best efforts, we will occasionally have a bad experience with a new person. With empathy, this rejection will be easier to understand. We realize that this person is not rejecting us, but is reacting to some previous events in his life. We were the first opportunity for this person to unload his negative luggage. Bad luck on our part. Unfortunately, his acidic verbal vomit is all over us.

It happens.

Think about our lives. Have we ever had a bad moment? Our treasured item breaks. Our home team loses. We get fired. The policeman writes that ticket while ignoring our pleas for leniency. Somehow, we think we are the only ones who have moments of extreme unhappiness. Unfortunately, everyone does.

Remember, we only see the top 15% of people's lives on social media. The remaining 85% of their lives isn't so rosy.

We don't want to judge our progress in meeting new people by these extreme moments. They happen. And they happen to everyone. We can let those moments stop us. Or, we can understand those people and their feelings, then continue to move forward to meet new people.

CONVERSATION BASICS.

This chapter will be short.

When meeting new people, we have many fears.

What will I say? Will I appear intelligent? What should I talk about? What will my conversation partner be thinking while I am talking?

Forget these worries. None of these worries apply.

Let me describe the perfect conversation from our conversation partner's eyes.

The perfect conversation.

Our conversation partner talks **at** us. We listen.

How to be popular?

We listen, while our conversation partner talks **at** us.

Conversation reality.

Why do people search us out as conversation partners? Because they want new people to talk at. They have already bored their previous conversation partners.

The only skill we need to know?

How to listen.

Bad advice.

"Eat less, exercise more." That is the worse weight-loss advice ever. Why? Because that isn't the reality for overweight people like me.

Scientifically true. Logically correct. But that isn't our reality. Look around. Proof is everywhere. Every overweight person has that wonderful advice already, and it hasn't made a difference.

Here is equally bad advice:

"Just talk to people."

When meeting new people, they don't want to be talked to. They want to talk.

That's it?

Easy. End of chapter.

LISTENING BASICS.

How do we feel when others don't listen to us? Do we resent it when others don't pay attention to us or to what we are saying?

We feel devalued and small.

When meeting someone for the first time, listening etiquette is mandatory. If we don't look like we are listening or paying attention, we are doomed.

What should we do and not do to appear as a good listener? Here are some ideas.

Listening: the big picture.

If we listen to hear and understand, our body language and replies reflect our good intentions. Our desire to hear and understand what the other person says will fix most body language problems.

But what does "listen to hear and understand" mean?

First, be curious. This focuses our attention.

Second, if we want to learn new perspectives, we try to understand the meaning of our partner's words. We want to internalize the message. We want to know how this message applies to us.

Here is the opposite. Our partner talks. We listen to the words only so we know what we can say next. We don't think about the message. Instead, we think about what we can say as soon as our partner shuts up. People notice this, and it doesn't look good.

Listening to understand the message, without worrying about what we can say next, works. We will look great in the eyes of others.

Unfortunately, most people communicate poorly. They don't listen to the other person. They are so caught up with the conversation inside of their heads that they communicate on autopilot. They talk as soon as there is a space in the conversation.

How ugly is this automatic communication?

Really ugly. And we tested it. Prepare for a shock.

I travel by air and meet dozens of staff members. Same with my hotel stays. I meet check-in staff at the desk in the lobby. Plus, I meet service staff when I go out to eat. And guess what all these staff members are paid to say?

"How are you today?"

They say these words so often that these words are automatic. They've lost their impact.

So, for years, this is how I've been answering the question, "How are you today?"

I reply, "I am fat."

Can you guess the responses to my reply?

Unfortunately, you already know. The staff doesn't hear or take notice of my reply. Instead they continue the conversation by asking for my last name, what would I like to order, etc.

They are used to people replying, "I am fine." They hear that reply so many times that they shut off the listening part of their brains after they ask, "How are you today?" They shut off their attention to my reply, so that they can think more about themselves. Embarrassing, but true.

Sometimes I have someone with me when checking in or ordering food. I warn them in advance to watch the response. We both have a good laugh about it later.

No one listens?

Well, not everyone ignores my reply, "I am fat." About two out of ten people look up and say, "Huh?" Yes, 80% of the people we talk to don't hear what we are saying.

What happens when someone notices my unusual reply? They smile. Then they lie to me by saying, "Oh, you are not fat." At least they are politically correct and polite.

The lesson we can take from this is that we must listen closely to what someone says. It is too easy to assume what someone else will say, and turn off our minds to the communication.

"One day closer to death."

What is another reason we should pay close attention to what others say?

Imagine this scenario. We meet a new person and say, "How are you today?"

He answers, "One day closer to death."

Ouch!

We reply, "Uh … uh … well, I guess you are not looking forward to tomorrow."

Do we want this person in our life? Probably not. But if we listened automatically, we wouldn't notice this depressing reply.

Now, everyone **talks** about listening, but that is the problem. It is all talk.

So how about some quick tips to help us listen better?

LISTENING TIPS TO MAKE US LOOK AWESOME.

We don't have to enroll in an expensive listening course to start listening better right now. With a few adjustments to our current way of thinking, we can be a better listener immediately.

Don't talk.

We know that people's favorite subject is themselves. That is all they want to talk about. Our lives? Not even a close second place.

The only reason most people want to talk is … to talk about themselves. When we talk, they feel we are stealing their talking time.

There is another problem with our talking. When we talk, we stop listening, and so does our conversation partner.

The best advice? Don't talk.

The power of the fist.

If you are seated, this is an easy way to be a better listener. Form a fist with one hand, place it under our chin, and then push up! This will keep our mouths from opening. It's a great conversation tool.

And what happens if we feel the urge to talk? Push our fist up harder!

People will say we are great conversation partners when we don't talk. That is what people are looking for in conversation. They talk. We listen.

And if we are afraid of "putting our foot in our mouth," then the fist technique prevents us from saying something stupid.

Approval?

People love approval. They dress for approval. They pose for approval. And if we give people approval when they talk, they will love us.

How do we give approval to someone without interrupting their monologue? By gently nodding. This signals to our conversation partner, "Yes. Please go on. You are so interesting. I agree with you, 100%. You are incredibly intelligent with your all-knowing wisdom."

Okay, slightly exaggerated, but nodding works.

However, don't overdo the nodding. That will look phony and staged.

Listen to hear, not to respond.

As we mentioned in the last chapter, if we listen to see what we can say next, our mind works hard on our witty reply. But wait! That means we are not thinking about the meaning of what our conversation partner is saying. It's as if we are not listening at all.

Will our partner notice this? Yes. And our partner will feel disrespected because we don't value his words.

This takes practice. It is not a natural skill. One quick way to improve faster is to say to ourselves, "I want to read 'between the lines' of what this person is saying."

By pretending we are a detective or investigator, our concentration improves. Try it. The added benefit is that it is fun.

One-upmanship stinks.

How does our partner feel when we minimize his accomplishments by saying we do more? Here is a sample of this type of conversation.

Partner: "I just went on a one-week cruise."

Us: "That's nothing! I go on a two-week cruise three times a year."

Partner: "On the cruise, I started to work out and get into shape."

Us: "I am training for the local marathon."

Partner: "I saved every month for the cruise."

Us: "Saving is for losers. I invest aggressively like the smart, rich people."

Partner: "Well, at least I had a good time on my cruise."

Us: "I had the best time. I sat at the Captain's table, took the best tours, and of course, I am a VIP member of the cruise line. I get special privileges too."

Our conversation partner wants to be the hero or heroine of the conversation. We irritate people by telling them that we are better. Everyone hates arrogant, self-absorbed conversation partners. It is impossible to build rapport when we try to top their stories.

Avoid the appearance of interrogation.

Remember those crime movies where the detectives badgered the poor prisoner? The detectives threw rapid-fire questions at the prisoner, hoping to break down the prisoner's defenses.

We don't want to sound like that. Too many questions too quickly might put some people on guard. Throw in a little pause before asking the next question. Make sure the questions relate to what our partner said, instead of sounding like the questions came from a prepared list.

Think how it would feel if someone asked us these questions in rapid succession:

- What is your name?
- Where do you live?
- How many children do you have?
- What are their ages?
- What time do they get out of school in the afternoon?

Uh-oh. This is getting too personal too fast. Doesn't feel good. A few pauses would help.

If we accidentally trigger the interrogation reaction from our partner, mention something about ourselves briefly. Then, of course, let our partner start talking again.

Prepare a list of emergency questions.

When possible, prepare ourselves with a list of emergency questions before meeting people. Why? If the conversation runs dry, the silence is deafening. Everyone feels embarrassed in these awkward moments.

If we know someone we would like to meet, ask ourselves, "What are three questions I could ask this person?"

These questions and answers will be interesting for us. Our conversation partner feels respected too.

What else can we do? How about a prepared list of easy questions designed to open up a conversation or keep it going? Having something we can always ask will make us feel more confident. Here is a starter list of these types of questions.

- "Where are the refreshments?"
- "Do you know where the toilets are located?"
- "I missed the first part of the event. Could you tell me what they covered?"
- "So how did you meet your spouse?"
- "Do you know the organizer?"
- "Where did you buy those shoes?"

- "Have you taken any trips recently?"
- "Do you know what time this event finishes?"

Our accomplishments are … nothing.

People don't care about all the great things we've accomplished. Why? Because they are not interested in us. They are interested in themselves. They're selfish! (Just like us.)

But what if we won the Nobel Peace Prize last week? No, no one wants to hear about it. Let's get over it.

If people are not interested in our wonderful accomplishments, then are they interested in our problems?

No! They are even less interested in our problems. No one wants to hear about our problems. Even psychologists that are paid to listen to problems want time off to rejuvenate.

- What if we had a flat tire on the way to the event? No, no one wants to hear about it.
- What if we survived a gruesome operation? No, no one wants to hear about it.
- What if we lost our arms fighting a dragon? No, no one wants to hear about it.

See a pattern?

So, what if we had a bad day, and we just want people to feel sorry for us?

No one wants to listen to our woes. We are interrupting their speaking time.

"How are you?"

Listen to those words closely. When I first tried meeting new people, I interpreted this question as, "Please tell me your entire life history." Wow. My interpretation was way off!

Our conversation partner wants us to reply, "Oh, I am fine. Enjoying this great day. And what about you?"

That should be the limit to our side of the conversation.

People want us to finish talking quickly, so they can get back to talking.

Be curious. Ask questions.

Asking questions is a great way to start a conversation with anyone. This also gives us an opportunity to learn. We become more well-rounded with the new things we learn. As an extra benefit, now we can participate more effectively in future conversations.

Think of all the great new things we can learn by listening to others. They have had experiences we could never have. They've met people we will never meet. What a great way to learn new things.

Just ask questions and listen.

We don't have to have an agenda with every person, every time. We don't have to try to make conditional friendships so that we can ask them a favor. And we don't have to be looking for an opportunity to sell everyone our latest idea or invention.

But … I am nervous. What will people think of me?

Remember? Stop talking about ourselves, and start thinking about others. When our focus is on others, we won't hear our inner voice saying, "I don't know what I am talking about. How do I look? Is my hair okay?"

Be curious a little longer. Ask a few more questions and let our conversation partner talk. When we focus on our conversation partner, we forget about ourselves and our issues.

What if we don't know how to reply?

Afraid of that pause when we don't know what to say? Don't worry. The pause seems forever to us, but to our conversation partner, it shows that we are thinking about what he said.

Good news: people are impatient. If we pause too long, they start talking again. They love filling dead space with more talking. So don't feel intimidated or rushed to make a reply.

Remember the definition of "small talk."

Small talk is allowing the other person to do all the talking, while we relax and listen.

Perhaps this is an exaggerated definition of small talk, but it is true. Most conversations are not exchanges of scientific research. Most conversations consist of one person talking all about himself. The other person patiently listens, avoiding interruption.

What about the initial conversation? The first few sentences when we meet someone?

The first few sentences are the way humans size each other up. For us, this is part of the rapport-building process. Our partner will form an opinion of us based on these first few words. Hopefully, this opinion will be positive. And then, our partner can talk, talk, and talk.

Remember, our conversation partner is checking us out. He wants to know if we will approve his monologue.

But what about our side of the conversation? We have great things to share with humanity.

We shouldn't worry that our wonderful information and amazing experiences will be bottled up inside of us forever. We might get our chance later. Maybe.

Most people have an internal program from their parents that says, "Don't talk all about yourself. Be polite. Let others talk also."

So be prepared. Say a few words about ourselves. Then, ask another question so our partner can continue talking.

What was your name?

In *How To Win Friends and Influence People*, Dale Carnegie taught us that people love hearing their names. But to do this, we have to remember their names. That is the hard part. Many gurus and experts have tricks and strategies to help. The approaches range from saying our conversation partner's name back to them quickly, to associating their name to something unusual to help our memory.

A few people are great at remembering names. Most aren't. The shortest advice we can give is to care about our conversation partner. That will help.

How important is remembering names? Ask ourselves, "How do we feel when someone calls us by the wrong name?"

Not good. It definitely doesn't make meeting people pleasant for either party. But don't despair. If we connect well, they might forgive us.

If we grew up in a large family, we remember our mother or father calling us by the wrong name often. Why? Having multiple children destroys parts of our brains. Anyway, we forgave them. Other people might forgive us too.

What should I talk about?

Try to keep our questions in context to our surroundings. If we are attempting to meet new people at a political rally, politics would be a good starting point. Asking what they do for hobbies may not be appropriate at this time.

We need to match the tone of the event also. At a memorial service, we wouldn't start by saying, "Hey, let's karaoke!" This statement would be appropriate at a fun and lighthearted party, not at a somber event.

What shouldn't I talk about?

If we want people to feel good around us, we don't want to talk about negative subjects. For example, we avoid that one person at work who always bring up the negative news. We don't feel good about our conversations when he starts by saying:

- "Did you hear about the tax increase coming up?"
- "Wow! I wonder how many people got injured in that accident?"
- "I can't believe how this politician is getting away with stealing money from our pockets. What are your thoughts?"
- "Did you watch the news last night?"
- "Did you see someone won the $60 million lottery? Horrible they have to pay taxes on it, what a rip-off."

Is there positive news out there? Yes, but our negative co-worker will never bring it up. He has an addiction to negativity. We don't want to be like him in our conversations with new people.

What if someone is "uninformed?"

Remember our empathy. When listening, we are under no obligation to accept everything our partner says as truth. Yes, some people do tell tall tales or are grossly inaccurate. This is not the time to correct them. We want to connect with them first. That is the purpose of meeting new people.

We don't have to form a new opinion or belief based on what others tell us. We don't even have to give them advice. Most times it is better to listen to the words they say and to make no comment.

Before I read Dale Carnegie's book, I felt obligated to correct every misstatement in my partners' conversations. I interfered with my partners' speaking time. A definite no-no. No wonder nobody wanted to talk to me, the human fact-checker.

What if someone has big problems? Should I help?

We started a conversation with a stranger. We are not psychologists. It is not up to us to solve their deep psychological problems. No one expects us to be the instant solution to their problems. Even if we could solve their problems, think of all the psychologists out of work! Who would pay for their big mortgages and swimming pools?

Plus, if we solve everyone's problems, they wouldn't have anything else to talk about in future conversations. Yes, some people want to keep their problems.

We are only looking to meet new people. Our current superpowers are limited to listening.

How about giving advice?

No. Don't do it. Don't even think about it.

Even if people ask for our advice, don't do it.

Why?

#1. People don't want our advice. Ever. They are already doing what they want to do.

#2. Our advice will conflict with the few facts they gave us. We don't know the whole story.

#3. People want approval. They don't want us telling them what they should do differently.

#4. People don't want us taking up their talking time with advice.

#5. We can't even begin to understand this person's life history, internal programs, etc. We don't have enough information.

#6. Our advice comes from our life history and programs. This isn't remotely close to the other person's experience.

#7. This isn't a good way to make a good first impression.

We get the point. While there may be exceptions, giving advice is generally a bad idea when we are trying to meet people.

But what if they beg me for advice?

Beware. This is a trap. They don't want advice. They only want approval for what they are doing already. Don't go there.

However, it is acceptable for us to ask them for advice. They love telling us what to do and how to fix our lives. Of course, we don't have to implement their advice.

What if they want to interrupt me?

Let them. They have stopped listening anyway. Watch for signs of impatience with our conversation partners. If they are anxious to interrupt us, we were probably boring them anyway. Let them talk about something more interesting – themselves, of course.

Can I interrupt them?

No.

We cannot interrupt our conversation partner. This is rude. Interrupting creates the following conversation in our conversation partner's head:

"You want to interrupt me? Are you telling me that my conversation is boring? Do you think that what you want to say now is more important than listening to me?"

Bad. Just bad. Yes, we hate standing there listening when we have something to say. But to interrupt? It only makes things worse.

So, what are we to do when we are stuck listening to a boring monologue from our conversation partner? Here are some options:

- Fake a heart attack. Let the paramedics take us out of this uncomfortable situation.

- Try to involve another person in the conversation. Then it is easier to say, "Excuse me. I need to slip away for one second."

- During one of our nods of approval, say, "Yes. Oh my, we should get in line now for the refreshments."
- Ask for a business card and comment, "Wow. This is a great card. Let me show it to my friend over there."

And sometimes, we are trapped. That is part of the price of meeting new people. We never know what we will experience until we meet them.

What if someone is rude?

Scratch them off our potential friends list. Who wants a friend that is rude to others?

We shouldn't prejudge their rudeness, since we don't know who talked to them before us. But, we should take a hint. When our partner gives short, one-word answers, he doesn't want to pursue our conversation. Maybe he is having a bad day.

The dangers of pretending to listen.

Don't pretend to listen so that we have a chance to talk about our agenda. By missing what other people say, we look bad. Here is an example.

Us: "How are you today?"

Conversation partner: "My mother just died."

Us: "Yeah. Did I tell you about the new car I am looking to buy?"

Well, our new car is definitely interesting to us. It dominates our brains. When we miss part of our partner's conversation, it could be embarrassing. Pay attention!

Start with light-hearted, non-invasive conversation.

Asking people about a recent holiday is safe.

Asking them about their marital status … not so safe.

Don't get personal too soon.

Initial conversations are not a good place to share intimate details. For instance, nobody wants to hear about our personal hygiene woes. Instead, they might want something more uplifting in our initial conversation.

When is a good time for us to speak?

In the beginning. And just briefly. Usually the word "Hi" will suffice. Then let the other person talk. We are just starting in our skill journey to meet new people. No need for us to have interesting things to say.

Won't people judge me and my lack of communication skills?

We don't have to be the world's greatest interviewer or conversationalist right away. People won't care too much. They just want to talk. We are there. They talk at us and they are happy. Problem solved.

But what happens when I have to talk?

What kind of questions could I ask next so my partner resumes talking?

Try to avoid questions that can be answered with one or two words. These are "closed" questions. For example, if our question can be answered with a simple "yes" or "no," it is a "closed" question.

Instead, ask open-ended questions that require a longer answer. That takes the pressure off us and gets our partner talking again.

Learning to ask open-ended and interesting questions is easy. Here are a few examples.

- "How did you feel about her speech?"
- "What is your opinion on this proposal?"
- "Could you explain how that works?"

We are looking for questions that have longer answers.

When talking about others.

When our partner asks our opinion about other people, be positive. If possible, make a compliment about the other person. If this compliment gets back to the other person, it will have ten times the effect than if we said it to that person directly.

Why do we avoid saying negative things about others? First, people like associating with positive people. Second, what if we say something negative about this person's acquaintance or friend? This could make the rest of our conversation go badly.

Keeping the conversation going.

One secret to new conversations is to find common ground. Sometimes our conversation partner will give us hints. Other times, we will have to guess. Here are some common questions that we can ask that help us locate common ground:

- "Do you have pets?"
- "Do you enjoy hot weather like we have this week?"
- "What is your favorite hobby?"
- "What is your favorite television show?"
- "How did you hear about this event?"
- "How did you meet the hostess?"

Yes, it can be hard to find common ground with some people. Fortunately, small talk is more about quantity than substance.

Later, once we are comfortable with each other, we can have deep and meaningful discussions.

If we have patience, we can eventually find something interesting about everyone we talk to. Even the most polar opposites have something interesting about them. Give everyone a chance. They may surprise us.

How to keep the other person talking.

Ever feel like we don't know what to say? Then our best strategy is to let the other person continue talking. Here are some "please continue with your brilliant conversation" phrases that we can use.

"A-ha, interesting! Wow! Tell me more."

"Hmmm, I see."

"What do you mean by that?"

"Got it."

"Uh-huh."

"Really?"

"How did you feel about that?"

"So then what happened?"

"How did that affect you?"

"Wow. That's hard to do."

"That is interesting."

"So what do you think will happen next?"

"I don't quite understand that. Could you explain more?"

"How can I help you?"

"Tell me more."

"Gee, how did you get by?"

"I am curious why you responded that way."

Why so many ways to keep people talking? So we can learn more. We are curious. It is hard to learn new things if **we** are talking. Other people have information, skills, and experiences that we don't. This is our chance to add them to our lives.

Body language clues.

At the subconscious level, people can detect if we are listening or waiting for our chance to talk. People always want to know what kind of agenda we have. Example of agendas:

- Men chatting up women to get a date.

- Salesmen pretending to be friendly to build trust with potential customers.

- Strangers looking for a new friend or someone to talk to at a party.

- College freshmen sorting through potential friends who have common interests.

- Politicians looking for influencers to help with re-election.

- People making conditional friendships so they can ask for a favor.

Listening is hard. Our mind wants to drift. We want to think and talk about our agenda.

So what clues do prospects pick up on when our mind is not on their conversation?

- Glazed look in our eyes.

- Blank expression.
- Nervousness while waiting.
- Delayed reactions to what they are saying, because we weren't listening to them.
- Glancing at people walking by.

Yawning would be a clue so obvious that even the conscious mind would pick that up.

How does our conversation partner feel? Annoyed? Devalued?

How would our conversation partner see us? Impolite? Uncaring? Selfish?

The point is, we should be curious. We should listen to hear and understand. We shouldn't listen only so we know what we can say next.

If we pay close attention to what our conversation partner is saying, we will get a great gift. Our partner will think we are charismatic.

And as a bonus, our conversation partner might believe that we are a genius like him.

Laugh at jokes.

When we laugh at other people's jokes, they feel good. And if we are making new friends, making them feel good is important.

What if their joke is not funny? It doesn't cost much to force ourselves to make a little laugh. The alternative is ugly.

Someone makes a joke, and we stare at them with a deadpan face. Yes, that should kill any connection that person felt with us.

If we find that we cannot laugh at jokes that aren't funny, now is a good time to practice in front of a mirror. We may need that reaction in our quest to meet new people.

Unfortunately, not everyone has the same taste when it comes to humor.

And finally, phone etiquette.

Our goal is to meet new people and have a conversation.

Our goal is not to be talking or using our phone.

If we are serious about meeting new people, we need to turn off our phones.

What? Yes, turn off our phones. It is legal. We won't be arrested. The world will still exist.

Why turn off our phones?

Let's practice our empathy. Imagine how we would feel in this situation.

A person approaches us and starts a conversation. During the conversation, he constantly checks his phone for messages. Maybe he even starts returning his phone messages.

How do we feel?

We feel that anything on this person's phone is more important than our conversation. Our value plummets to zero! Even the lowest-level message or notification has more value to this person than we do. This is not going to end well.

What is next?

We have enough listening tips now to make us a professional. To others, we will appear to be the most awesome conversation partner in the history of humanity. They will love us. They will be glad that we started a conversation with them.

But let's move on and take a brief look at rapport. We will need this to keep our conversations moving forward.

BUILDING RAPPORT.

Rapport comes after we make that initial contact and start our conversation. Building rapport is natural for most of us.

For example, one of the ways to build rapport is to find something in common. We already do this when we meet someone new. See if this conversation sounds familiar to you.

Our conversation partner says, "I am from Omaha."

And if we can, how do we naturally respond?

We say, "I know somebody from Omaha." Or, "I drove through Omaha once 22 years ago on my way to a conference."

Somehow, we know to look for commonalities to connect with people. We look for:

- People we know in common.
- Places we both visited.
- Similar tastes in food.
- Liking the same team.
- Common excitement over department store sales.
- Experiences we both enjoy.

The key word is "common."

We already have something in common.

One way of looking at rapport is that we both are on the same side of an issue or belief. We think the same.

Does this mean we have to agree 100%? No. Maybe our rapport is that we both believe in being open-minded. We believe that others can have valid opinions that are different from ours.

But most times, rapport will mean that we think the same way. That is why we desperately seek out something in common when we talk to a new person.

But here is the good news. We are already on the same side of something. What do we have in common? Well, we and the person we meet both chose to be … here.

- If it is a political rally, we have our political views in common.

- If it is a sale at the local department store, we both love sales.

- If it is a "how to invest in real estate" seminar, we share our excitement about investing.

- If it is a festival, we both came to have fun and socialize. What could be easier?

When we have something in common, then building rapport is easy. All we need to do is remember what brought us to this event.

Anti-rapport?

When first meeting people, we should take avoid talking about religion, politics, sports, and health remedies. People have strong beliefs on these topics.

For example, if we get 100 nutritionists in a room, we will have 100 different opinions on what we should do for our health. All will claim they are right, and the other 99 are misinformed idiots. Well, maybe not that bad, but close.

It is okay for us to listen. We can stay in rapport if we listen.

But offering our opinion? This could be the start of leaving our rapport behind. Yes, we will meet new people, but only one time. They will avoid future contact with us.

Rapport is easy.

If we avoid disagreement, and look for commonalities, we will do fine when we meet new people.

So for now, let's just concentrate on our main goal, meeting new people. There are many good books on building rapport. We wrote one of those books: *How To Get Instant Trust, Belief, Influence and Rapport! 13 Ways To Create Open Minds By Talking To The Subconscious Mind.*

Feeling ninja-like in our listening skills?

We should. These commonsense guidelines will help us listen better and bond with our new conversation partner.

But what about mirroring, modeling, NLP techniques, ninja eye contact and conversational hypnosis?

Sure, we can learn more about listening and building rapport. We always want to improve. But let's not put off talking to people by hiding behind the excuse that we need more training.

For now, we want to meet new people.

Let's move on to some group guidelines.

BASIC GROUP RULES.

Enter a room full of strangers. Could this be the number one fear in our lives? Oh, it could be worse. What if we had to make a speech to this group? Now, that would be much worse!

A room full of strangers challenges our social skills. Our social skills may be weak. Why?

We lost much of our ability to meet and talk to people with the growth of technology. We replaced talking to someone on the telephone with email, messaging, and texting. We shop online in our pajamas. We don't go to the local shopping mall. We avoid people and the crowds.

When was the last time we talked to a bank teller? Now we go to the ATM, or do our banking online.

It is time to brush up on some social skills.

Our comfort zone.

If we are an introvert, we gravitate toward what is most comfortable. Meeting new people isn't easy.

At a party or group gathering, if we connect with a new person, we will want to stay with that person. But how will our new contact feel if we monopolize his or her time for the entire evening? Not good. We will appear needy and clingy. Our new contact might feel that we have no other friends.

We don't want to, but we have to break away. This gives our conversation partner a break from us.

The good news is that this gives us a chance to meet yet another new person at this gathering.

Smile in the face of stress.

If we want to meet people in a group, yes, it will be more challenging. In groups, some people are close friends. They form a closed circle and their body language appears to close us out of their conversations. Other people look intimidating. Maybe we don't feel we will have a lot in common with that tattoo-collecting biker by the bar.

Even though we are uneasy, we can change our perspective. That is within our control. A little mindset adjustment helps.

We can still smile and try to approach new people by thinking, "Hey, they want to meet new people too! They didn't come to this party to be alone."

Try to find "loners" first.

Check the walls. Most lone party-goers will try to blend into the background and lean against the walls. They will stare at their text messages, or try to appear inconspicuous. They would be thrilled to have someone to talk to. It's embarrassing to be alone at a party or group gathering. They don't want to look like the only person at the party with no friends.

Feeling like a loner is not a good feeling. This could be our "good deed" for the day also. Now our chances of meeting someone are better.

Use the opening words we learned earlier. The nice thing is that we are meeting one person, not an entire group. And, this person is glad to talk to us.

When we approach this person, remember he doesn't know us and will make instant judgments about us. Now is not the time for bad body language. Nor is this the time for an invasive first question.

We want to start with an easy question just to check this person's temperature. An easy question could be something as simple as, "Do you know where the hostess is?" Or, "Could you direct me to the toilets?"

When he answers the question, we can gauge if he wants to continue a conversation with us or not. Watch for one-word answers from frowning people who look like they are recovering from hemorrhoid surgery. That is a hint.

If we meet one person at a time, soon we will have many contacts at the party or event. In fact, we will be popular with the other introverts!

Why start with lone individuals first? Because it is intimidating to walk up to a closed group of friends. Trying to enter an ongoing conversation among close friends is hard.

Remember, we don't have to meet everyone at the party. That should remove some stress.

Want another group strategy?

Who organized this party or event?

If we go to an event, find the organizer and volunteer to help. Most organizers appreciate all the help they can get. We can offer to help at the registration desk. This gives us the perfect excuse to say "Hi" to everyone. We won't be a stranger later when we visit with them. Or, offer to help pass out materials.

What about parties?

Find the host or hostess, and offer to help. We could take a tray of appetizers around the room and offer them to guests. This is a great way to make our initial impression not only on the host or hostess, but also everyone at the party. It's a natural way to meet people, and we won't feel so shy. And with luck, we will meet everyone at the party within the first hour.

Stay in sync when entering group conversations.

What if we do want to join in with a group of strangers? When joining a group, make sure we are fully aware of the current conversation. Yes, it is a good idea to listen a bit before talking. Here is an example of being out of sync with group conversations.

A group is talking about a recent disaster in the city. We jump into the conversation by saying, "I love collecting shirts with cat photos. Have you seen any good ones lately?"

The group feels like someone is dragging fingernails across a chalkboard.

Use common sense. We would like to contribute and enhance current conversations if we are in a group.

What if the group has strong opinions?

Is it safe to talk and share our opinions with these opinionated strangers?

We want to avoid opinions about people. But events? We can risk an opinion safely if:

1. If the entire group complains, we can offer our negative comment.

2. If the entire group loves an event, we can offer our positive comment.

If we have any doubts, don't risk rejection and embarrassment. Say, "Wow. This is interesting. I didn't know all these things. What do you think about it?"

Yes, pass the conversation along to someone else … quickly. We want to meet new people. Now is not the time to convert new people to our positions on everything.

So let's move on. We know what to do when we meet new people. Now, let's find some new people to talk to.

Finding new people.

Exhausted our personal contacts?

We can go anywhere to meet new people. But let's be smart about our search.

If we look for new people in positive environments, we tend to meet positive people. If we look for new people in negative environments, we tend to meet negative people.

Which is a better choice? Choosing to attend a self-improvement event or a late-night excursion to a bar with depressed people?

Want to feel comfortable when finding new people? Go to places where people have interests similar to ours. At least we will have more to talk about when we meet someone.

Where do I find special people?

People are everywhere.

That is not the challenge. The challenge is inside of our heads. Yes, it is a mindset. There isn't a reported drought of humans near us.

If we feel like there is no one to talk to in our location, this is a good time to change that thinking.

We are the location. Yes, everywhere we go, there are people around us.

Possibly we think that there are no **approachable** people.

Ah, now that is something different. If we don't know how to approach people, then that mindset will always stay the same. Fortunately, we learned how to approach people already. And, we can choose which people we want to approach.

Who do I approach first?

Since we are going to initiate the contact, we can choose where we look for new people.

Jim Rohn is famous for saying, "We are the average of the five people we spend the most time with."

This prompts a great question. If we can choose which people we want to meet, who would we like to spend time with?

If we associate with people who are positive and confident, it will start rubbing off on us. When we are looking to meet someone new, which qualities and traits would we like them to have? We can control what we look for.

Think about going to a party. Who do people want to mingle with? People who are negative? Or people who are positive?

Of course, the positive people. They have more uplifting stories. They talk about where they are going. They have goals and dreams. And, they are looking at the best side of things.

The negative people? They want people to feel sorry for them and blame the world for their woes. Or they attack other people's reputations to feel better about themselves. If we are trying to change ourselves for the better, we should avoid these negative people. If they become friends, they will rub off on us!

Now, let's find some people.

Social groups.

Instead of being a loner at a party, we could go to a local social group that has a common hobby. For example, if we like eating, there may be a "dinner group" that meets monthly at restaurants. Each meeting takes place at a new restaurant to try their food. Yes, we will meet the same people over and over, but they love meeting and socializing over food. If this is our passion, we could join several dinner groups. We just have to watch our waistlines.

On the Internet, it isn't hard to find an interest group that resonates with us. For example, if you love the idea of RV camping, you don't have to own a camper to participate in the group. Non-RV owners are welcomed to the group.

Book clubs? A bit quieter. Members get together to discuss the latest book of choice. Definitely a safe place to meet new people. Of course, this group may be less outgoing than other groups. Same with groups that meet to play board games.

Belly dancing? Some of us have more belly than we need. It would be good to exercise with others in a fun activity. But, joining a volleyball group would put us in contact with more outgoing people.

There are groups for music, art, outdoor activities, fashion, movies, fitness, photography, learning new languages and more. There are even Harry Potter enthusiast groups in some cities. Surely there are a few groups that we would love to be part of.

Learning opportunities.

People and companies offering private courses often have free evening previews. Whether the courses are for personal development or investing, one thing is certain. The people attending this evening preview event will be positive, and looking forward to the future. These are great people to meet.

Look for classes or preview sessions on investing, budgeting, relationships, selling, finance … the choices are unlimited. Surrounding ourselves with positive people who want to learn means that we will meet open-minded people.

Afraid of public speaking?

Almost everyone is. Some claim that public speaking is a fate worse than death.

Toastmasters is famous for helping people overcome their fear of public speaking. Here is a chance to learn a new skill while meeting other people on a weekly basis. We get to know the members of our group quite well. We hear them talk about their personal experiences every week.

There is a common bond with the group. We overcome our fear and gain new skills together.

Networking groups.

In business, networking groups are common. Creating new contacts is the lifeblood of expanding businesses. While there are high-level networking groups that connect people with highly-specialized skills, we will want to participate in more general groups. For example, if we are a small business owner, the Chamber of Commerce has monthly get-togethers. Every person in that group attends for the sole purpose of meeting someone new. How easy is that?

There are plenty of informal networking groups outside of the Chamber of Commerce. Again, everyone attending wants to meet new people. That means they want to meet us. And we don't even need a business card to participate.

Some groups are quite formal with dues and rules, for instance, the BNI networking group. This is a group of small businesses that meet for breakfast solely for the purpose of creating new leads for each other.

However, there is nothing stopping us from starting our own small business networking group. We could even create a group with no dues. Keith and I wrote a book on how to do this: *Start SuperNetworking! 5 Simple Steps to Creating Your Own Personal Networking Group.*

Parties?

When going to a party, in the beginning, go with a friend. At worst, we will have someone to talk to. At best, we can invite someone into our conversation.

Parties can be after-work gatherings, birthday celebrations, going-away and coming-back events. Need more ideas?

How about a holiday BBQ or a housewarming event? Be creative. What is nice about parties is that everyone is in a festive mood. It's easy to start conversations with new people when they are happy. If we organize the event, everyone will want to talk to us.

Do we travel?

Traveling guarantees that we will be in contact with new people. Let's take advantage of this opportunity.

If we are in a travel environment, the people around us may be travelers too. Not only do we have something in common, they might want to meet new people also.

Here are some interesting questions that we can use to start and keep our conversation going.

- "What is the best thing to see while I'm visiting the city?"
- "What is something I must do while visiting the city?"
- "Where is the best place to eat here?"

- "Do you have any recommendations of the best places to stay?"
- "Where have you come from today? Have you traveled far?"
- "Do you know where I can find …?"
- "Do you know anyone here?"

These are easy, light-hearted questions that no one will find invasive.

Reunions?

Family reunions. Our relatives marry people we don't know. We can make it a point to welcome them and help introduce them to the other family members. That wasn't so hard.

Class reunions? We could organize an impromptu class reunion. Or, suggest the impromptu class reunion to our super-social classmate. He or she could organize the event with our help.

And guess who comes to the reunions? People we know, but they also come with their new spouses. Again, we can ease these new people into the group by introducing them to others.

Attend a home show expo.

Every year, many cities have home show expos. Hundreds of vendors display their newest and best ideas to thousands of visitors. Most people rush by every booth. The vendors struggle to talk to individuals because many people are afraid of being pressured.

We can practice talking with these vendors during their downtime. Plus, we could be helping them by making their booth look busy.

Flea markets.

Every city has them. Hundreds of people look forward to their weekends, bargain hunting at their favorite local flea markets. Who can we talk to there?

The vendors, of course. If we are interested in exotic sheepskin rugs from Peru, we will naturally meet other people at that booth. Already, we have a common interest. Oh, and don't forget the food stands. What do we have in common with everyone in line at the food stands? Food! It is easy to talk about how hungry we are, or how this stand makes the best hot dogs in the world.

Social media.

Meeting people online is not the same as meeting them in person. We can call this the "lite" version of meeting people.

Some people do this to the extreme. They have 5,000 imaginary friends on Facebook. Do they really know any of them? No.

This should give us a hint. We want quality contacts and relationships instead of simply clicking a button that says we are friends. And how will we create a deeper relationship with these initial contacts? With the same techniques we learned earlier in this book. Non-invasive questions, listening, etc.

Here is an easy online strategy. Ask ourselves this question: "If I have a choice, would I like to meet someone far away, or someone locally?"

The answer? If we meet people locally, we can eventually meet them in person at an event or over coffee at the local bistro. Because we've met them online already, we won't feel intimidated when we meet them in person.

Is there anything wrong with meeting someone far away? No. Who doesn't want to have friends from Nepal? Or Paraguay? It is just harder to meet them in person to build a deeper relationship.

When is social media a good time to practice meeting people? When we can't go out and meet people in person. This could be late at night when the children are in bed. Or, if we are still gathering our courage to meet someone in person, we can practice online.

Another online strategy is to contact people with similar interests. There are many places online where people of similar interests gather. Let's start there where we will have the best chance of building rapport.

Night classes.

We don't have to get a university degree to go to night school. Most communities have free or inexpensive night classes on a variety of subjects. What subject should we choose?

The subject that we are most interested in. Why? Because everyone else in our class will have something in common with us.

What a great place to meet new people. We will see them at every class. That familiarity will make conversations easy.

And as an extra bonus, we will learn new things about one of our favorite subjects.

Helping people.

So many people need help, and so few people are willing to help them. We can be one of those people. When we offer to help, it is easier to make a friend.

The opportunity to help people is always present. Think of the daily opportunities we have. We can help someone carry packages, or help someone clean up when a meeting is over. Or at parties, we can stay behind and help the host or hostess clean up.

Schools, volunteer organizations, and charities welcome anyone who offers to help. Anyone means … us. Not only do we get a chance to practice and meet new people, but we also make the world a better place for everyone.

Fundraisers? Well, we don't have to be the one to ask strangers for money. Don't panic. There are other duties we can do to help the fundraising organization.

Another side effect of helping people? We feel better about ourselves. To contribute to someone's happiness creates good feelings inside us. These feelings show in our outward appearance when we meet others. Now we are even more attractive to others.

Dance and self-defense classes.

Do we like to dance? Or, would we like to learn to dance? Dance classes force us to meet new people. Going by ourselves, we can balance out the other singles. The more, the merrier.

What about self-defense classes? The good news is that we see the same people every week. It won't be hard to strike up a conversation with them over time.

Like reading books?

Instead of reading books at home, why not join a local library reading group? We meet the same people weekly as we discuss new books. Easy.

Many book readers are introverted. We should feel comfortable in this environment.

Break up our routine.

If we keep going to the same places, and keep our current habits, we limit our chances of meeting new people. Focus on the word "variety" when choosing where to meet new people.

Get a haircut.

Beauticians and barbers are masters of communication. They can hold conversations with anyone, even the most inhibited, shy introvert.

There is no law that requires us to see the same beautician or barber every time we need a haircut. Why not vary our routine? We can meet someone new and have an immediate and relaxed conversation every time we need a haircut.

Could we improve this idea? Yes. Schedule our haircut on a busy day. Then, come one hour early by mistake, and have the chance to visit with other people who are waiting for their turn. What do we have in common? We all need a haircut.

Go for a walk.

Don't walk alone. Choose a walking path that is popular with the locals. Walkers are friendly. Plus, our added benefit is that we get exercise.

But how do we start that conversation with the other walkers? If we are afraid to start a conversation, here is a shortcut.

Get a dog. It is impossible to walk a dog without someone starting a conversation.

What if we don't own a dog? No problem. We can borrow a dog. Many dog owners would love to have us walk their dog.

What is a better conversation-starter than a dog? A baby. Babies are guaranteed to start conversations. Unfortunately, they are harder to borrow from their parents.

Get lost.

Now we have an excuse to ask directions. People are polite to lost travelers. What do we need directions to?

- To the toilets.
- To the garage sale.
- To the new store opening.
- To the registration table.

If we mess up our conversation with the person giving us directions, relax. We won't be seeing that person again for a while.

Finding people is easy.

Finding people to talk to is easy … if we have the skills.

Finding people to talk to is difficult when we don't have these simple skills.

So, feeling better about talking to new people?

Every time we approach another new person for conversation, we build our skill level. Soon, fear will only be a memory.

So, let's meet new people now!

And it is okay to start with the easy ones first. We will keep getting better and better.

THANK YOU.

Thank you for purchasing and reading this book. I hope you found some ideas that will work for you.

Before you go, would it be okay if I asked a small favor? Would you take just one minute and leave a sentence or two reviewing this book online? Your review can help others choose what they will read next. It would be greatly appreciated by many fellow readers.

I travel the world 240+ days each year.
Let me know if you want me to stop in your
area and conduct a live Big Al training.

→ **BigAlSeminars.com** ←

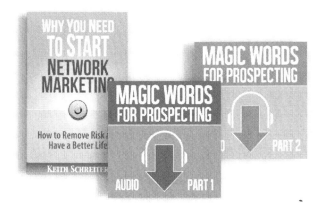

FREE Big Al Training Audios
Magic Words for Prospecting
plus Free eBook and the Big Al Report!

→ **BigAlBooks.com/free** ←

MORE BIG AL BOOKS

BIGALBOOKS.COM

Why Are My Goals Not Working?
Color Personalities for Network Marketing

Setting goals that work for us is easy when we have guidelines and a checklist.

Closing for Network Marketing
Getting Prospects Across The Finish Line

Here are 46 years' worth of our best closes. All of these closes are kind and comfortable for prospects, and rejection-free for us.

Pre-Closing for Network Marketing
"Yes" Decisions Before The Presentation

Instead of selling to customers with facts, features and benefits, let's talk to prospects in a way they like. We can now get that "yes" decision first, so the rest of our presentation will be easy.

The One-Minute Presentation
Explain Your Network Marketing Business Like A Pro

Learn to make your business grow with this efficient, focused business presentation technique.

Retail Sales for Network Marketers
How to Get New Customers for Your MLM Business

Learn how to position your retail sales so people are happy to buy. Don't know where to find customers for your products and services? Learn how to market to people who want what you offer.

Getting "Yes" Decisions
What insurance agents and financial advisors can say to clients

In the new world of instant decisions, we need to master the words and phrases to successfully move our potential clients to lifelong clients. Easy … when we can read their minds and service their needs immediately.

3 Easy Habits For Network Marketing
Automate Your MLM Success

Use these habits to create a powerful stream of activity in your network marketing business.

Motivation. Action. Results.
How Network Marketing Leaders Move Their Teams

Learn the motivational values and triggers our team members have, and learn to use them wisely. By balancing internal motivation and external motivation methods, we can be more effective motivators.

The Four Color Personalities for MLM
The Secret Language for Network Marketing

Learn the skill to quickly recognize the four personalities and how to use magic words to translate your message.

Ice Breakers!
How To Get Any Prospect To Beg You For A Presentation

Create unlimited Ice Breakers on-demand. Your distributors will no longer be afraid of prospecting, instead, they will love prospecting.

How To Get Instant Trust, Belief, Influence and Rapport!
13 Ways To Create Open Minds By Talking To The Subconscious Mind

Learn how the pros get instant rapport and cooperation with even the coldest prospects. The #1 skill every new distributor needs.

First Sentences for Network Marketing
How To Quickly Get Prospects On Your Side

Attract more prospects and give more presentations with great first sentences that work.

How to Follow Up With Your Network Marketing Prospects
Turn Not Now Into Right Now!

Use the techniques in this book to move your prospects forward from "Not Now" to "Right Now!"

How To Prospect, Sell And Build Your Network Marketing Business With Stories

If you want to communicate effectively, add your stories to deliver your message.

26 Instant Marketing Ideas To Build Your Network Marketing Business

176 pages of amazing marketing lessons and case studies to get more prospects for your business immediately.

How To Build Network Marketing Leaders
Volume One: Step-By-Step Creation Of MLM Professionals

This book will give you the step-by-step activities to actually create leaders.

How To Build Network Marketing Leaders
Volume Two: Activities And Lessons For MLM Leaders

You will find many ways to change people's viewpoints, to change their beliefs, and to reprogram their actions.

51 Ways and Places to Sponsor New Distributors
Discover Hot Prospects For Your Network Marketing Business

Learn the best places to find motivated people to build your team and your customer base.

Big Al's MLM Sponsoring Magic
How To Build A Network Marketing Team Quickly

This book shows the beginner exactly what to do, exactly what to say, and does it through the eyes of a brand-new distributor.

Public Speaking Magic
Success and Confidence in the First 20 Seconds

By using any of the three major openings in this book, we can confidently start our speeches and presentations without fear.

Worthless Sponsor Jokes
Network Marketing Humor

Here is a collection of worthless sponsor jokes from 25 years of the "Big Al Report." Network marketing can be enjoyable, and we can have fun making jokes along the way.

How To Get Kids To Say Yes!
Using the Secret Four Color Languages to Get Kids to Listen

Turn discipline and frustration into instant cooperation. Kids love to say "yes" when they hear their own color-coded language.

BigAlBooks.com

About the Authors

Keith Schreiter has 20+ years of experience in network marketing and MLM. He shows network marketers how to use simple systems to build a stable and growing business.

So, do you need more prospects? Do you need your prospects to commit instead of stalling? Want to know how to engage and keep your group active? If these are the types of skills you would like to master, you will enjoy his "how-to" style.

Keith speaks and trains in the U.S., Canada, and Europe.

Tom "Big Al" Schreiter has 40+ years of experience in network marketing and MLM. As the author of the original "Big Al" training books in the late '70s, he has continued to speak in over 80 countries on using the exact words and phrases to get prospects to open up their minds and say "YES."

His passion is marketing ideas, marketing campaigns, and how to speak to the subconscious mind in simplified, practical ways. He is always looking for case studies of incredible marketing campaigns that give usable lessons.

As the author of numerous audio trainings, Tom is a favorite speaker at company conventions and regional events.

Made in the USA
San Bernardino, CA
09 January 2020

62918789R00066